SAN DIEGO
C H A R G E R S

R I C H A R D   R A M B E C K

C R E A T I V E ⦿ E D U C A T I O N   I N C .

Published by Creative Education, Inc.
123 S. Broad Street, Mankato, Minnesota 56001

Designed by Rita Marshall

Cover illustration by Lance Hidy Associates

Photos by Allsport USA, Bettmann Archives, David Madison
Photography, Duomo, Focus On Sports, Spectra-Action,
Sportschrome and Third Coast

Library of Congress Cataloging-in-Publication Data

Rambeck, Richard.
  San Diego Chargers/Richard Rambeck.
  p.   cm.
  ISBN 0-88682-382-X
  1. San Diego Chargers (Football team)—History.   I. Title.
GV956.S29R36   1990
796.332′64′09794985—dc20   90-41207
                                             CIP

For the most part, major cities in the United States either are growing very slowly or are actually losing population. One notable exception is San Diego, which has grown from a good-sized city into the sixth largest metropolis in the country. San Diego is now the second most populous city in California, with more than 1.1 million people. Forty years ago, the city had less than 350,000 residents.

Why is San Diego booming? The weather is one good reason. San Diego has perhaps the most sunny, yet mild, climate of any major city in the United States. But San

The 50 yard line at Jack Murphy Stadium.

Paul Lowe was the Chargers' touchdown leader with ten TDs during the season.

Diego is more than just a place to go for sun and temperatures in the seventies and eighties year-round. San Diego has become a busy port city. It is home to one of the largest U.S. Navy bases in the country. The city is also known for such attractions as the world-famous San Diego Zoo and Marineland.

Excitement and fun, that's San Diego. It's also a good description of the city's professional football team, the Chargers. For thirty years, the San Diego Chargers—the guys with the lightning bolts on their helmets—have entertained their fans with high-powered offenses highlighted by one of the league's most explosive passing attacks. The lightning bolts are perfect for the team and the great quarterbacks who have led the Chargers' relentless aerial attack over the last three decades. Quarterbacks Jack Kemp, Tobin Rote, John Hadl, and Dan Fouts have zapped the rest of the league by unleashing the lightning in their powerful arms.

The Chargers have also been known for coaches who love to use the pass. San Diego's first coach, Sid Gillman, had built a National Football League championship team with the Los Angeles Rams by relying on the pass. In 1959 Gillman and the Rams parted company after a couple of losing seasons. Despite that, several teams wanted to hire Gillman as coach. The team that did was the Los Angeles Chargers, a first-year team in the new American Football League. The Los Angeles owner, millionaire Barron Hilton, believed that Gillman was the key to a successful franchise. Hilton must have known something, because the experts made the Chargers the favorites to win the AFL title in 1960—before the team had a single player under contract.

A high powered offense and a crushing defense is a Charger tradition.

Keith Lincoln was San Diego's top punt returner— averaging over twenty-one yards per carry.

Gillman signed the team's first two offensive stars: halfback Paul Lowe and quarterback Jack Kemp. Both would have an immediate impact, especially Lowe. In the Chargers' first preseason game—their first game ever— Lowe took the opening kickoff five yards deep in the end zone. About fifteen seconds later, Lowe was standing in the other end zone. The first play in the history of the Chargers covered 105 yards and netted the team six points. It was a great start, and the excitement would continue. Behind Lowe and Kemp, the Chargers won the AFL Western Division with a 10-4 record. Unfortunately, the team lost to the Houston Oilers 24-16 in the league title game. It was to be the last game played by the Los Angeles Chargers.

Barron Hilton owned a thrilling team. However, the Chargers didn't exactly own the hearts of Los Angeles fans. The L.A. Rams of the NFL were top dogs in Los Angeles, so Hilton decided to move his team down the California coast to San Diego. The San Diego Chargers were born, and Sid Gillman set out to make sure that the team's new city would have plenty of stars to cheer. Gillman managed to sign such great college players as running back Keith Lincoln and defensive linemen Earl Faison and Ernie Ladd, all of whom had been wanted dearly by teams in the NFL. These new standouts teamed with holdovers Jack Kemp, Paul Lowe, and powerful offensive lineman Ron Mix to lead the first-year San Diego Chargers to the Western Division title in 1961 with a 12-2 record. But for the second straight year, the Chargers were defeated by Houston in the AFL championship game, this time 10-3.

ALWORTH PROVES TO BE ALL-WORLD

Before the start of the 1962 season, the Chargers got Lance Alworth, a shifty wide receiver, in a trade. Alworth was a great athlete with speed, jumping ability, and the coordination of a gymnast. But his boyish appearance made him look more like a ball boy than an all-league receiver. "He first showed up at our office in June, looking for an apartment," said Al LoCasale, a Chargers' executive. "He had a skinhead haircut—he looked fifteen years old. Barbara, my secretary, said 'We're not giving you the money because we're not getting the paper.' She thought he was the newspaper boy."

Alworth, of course, wasn't the paperboy, but he also wasn't healthy during much of the 1962 season. Neither were a lot of San Diego's stars. Paul Lowe also was hurt. In fact, no less than twenty-three players missed at least two games for the Chargers, who slumped to a 4-10 record. The following year, Lowe and Alworth were healthy again, and Gillman brought in a new quarterback, the veteran Tobin Rote. Jack Kemp had been traded to Buffalo, and young John Hadl was having some trouble adjusting to pro football. So Gillman saw the need to have an old hand to steady the ship.

The San Diego coach couldn't have asked for a steadier hand than Rote's, who wound up leading the AFL in passing in 1963 with 2,510 yards and twenty touchdowns. Rote was clicking, and so was Alworth, who caught at least one touchdown pass in each of nine straight games in 1963. "In every huddle," Gillman recalled, "Lance would insist

1 9 6 3

Accuracy! Quarterback Tobin Rote completed nearly sixty percent of his passes.

A catch Lance Alworth would be proud of, (pages 10–11).

to the quarterback, 'I've got the up! I've got the up!' " That meant Alworth believed he had learned how to break free from his defender on the "up" or "fly" pattern, which was meant to carry the length of the field. "He always wanted the ball," Gillman said of Alworth. "He never got it enough. He was like a virtuoso, a violinist, playing his own music out there."

Alworth's amazing play earned him a new nickname, "Bambi." The Chargers called Alworth that because of his running style, which resembled a deer's. "Bambi, I used to love to watch him line up and take his stance," said Al LoCasale, "his free hand shaking, all the adrenaline pumping, all that energy waiting to explode." Alworth wasn't the only Charger ready to explode. The offense averaged more than twenty-eight points per game as the team moved into first place in the Western Division. Late in the season, Rote developed arm trouble, so Gillman handed the reins to Hadl. The young quarterback threw five touchdown passes in a 47-23 victory over Denver that clinched the division title.

Rushing leader Paul Lowe recorded over 1100 yards for the season.

The Chargers were underdogs to the Boston Patriots in the AFL championship game that was played in Boston. If the Chargers feared the Patriots, they certainly didn't show it. San Diego tallied three touchdowns in the first quarter. Rote scored on a short run, and then Keith Lincoln followed with a sixty-seven yard gallop. Paul Lowe closed the quarter with a fifty-eight yard run. San Diego wound up winning 51-10 as Lincoln rushed for 206 yards, and Hadl and Rote combined to pass for 285 yards.

HADL HANDLES THE PASSING ATTACK

The Chargers had won their first championship. Surprisingly, the team would not win another. San Diego captured Western Division titles in 1964 and 1965, but lost both years to the Buffalo Bills in the league championship game. The key player for the Chargers was John Hadl, who took over the starting quarterback position in 1964. Hadl, who had been a star at the University of Kansas, had a strong arm. But he also wasn't afraid to scramble around in the pocket and, if necessary, run with the ball.

Hadl's trademark became the late-game drive to pull out a victory. "I call him Cliff-hanger Hadl," Gillman said. "If a game goes down to the final minute, John is the best guy in the league at pulling something out of the hat." In 1965 "Cliff-hanger" led the AFL in passing with 2,798 yards and twenty touchdowns, many of them to the speedy

New home! San Diego stadium was dedicated before a crowd of 45,988 fans.

Alworth. Alworth, in fact, had the best year of his remarkable career, as he accumulated 1,602 yards pass receiving, a team record that still stands.

Unfortunately for Hadl and Alworth, their heroics couldn't produce another division championship. Defensive stars Ernie Ladd and Earl Faison were no longer with the team. As a result, San Diego gave up more than twenty points per game in 1966. The Chargers slumped to third place in the division with a 7-6-1 record. Despite the team's drop, Hadl and Alworth remained an explosive combination. Between them they owned virtually every San Diego passing record. "All the records are great," Hadl said, "but San Diego fans deserve a championship."

But San Diego was no longer a championship-caliber team. From 1967 through 1969, the high-scoring Chargers managed winning seasons every year. However, the team could not equal the records of the Oakland Raiders and Kansas City Chiefs. Both were powers in the Western Division, so San Diego settled for third every season. Even though the team couldn't rise to the top, Alworth and Hadl stayed there. Alworth led the league in receiving yardage in both 1968 and 1969, and Hadl was among the leaders in passing yardage every year.

In 1970 the AFL and NFL merged. The Chargers were placed in the Western Division of the American Football Conference along with Oakland, Kansas City, and the Denver Broncos. While the Chiefs and Raiders were Super Bowl contenders, the Chargers were headed the other way. In ten seasons in the AFL, San Diego had won one league title and five division championships, and had only

Another great wide receiver, Anthony Miller (#83).

Running back Mike Garrett was the club's rushing leader with over 1000 yards for the season.

one losing season. But the team had gotten old. Paul Lowe and Keith Lincoln weren't around anymore. Neither was Sid Gillman, who quit during the 1969 season.

After a 5-6-3 season in 1970, the Chargers traded Alworth to the Dallas Cowboys. The only longtime Charger left was Hadl. Even the owner was new; Eugene Klein was now the team's majority shareholder. The coach was new as well, but he was not new to the Chargers. Gillman returned as coach in 1971, but he and Klein didn't get along. After coaching the first ten games in 1971, Gillman decided he had had enough. Harland Svare, the team's general manager, took over as coach. Svare, unlike Gillman, was a defensive-oriented coach. However, as head coach for San Diego, Svare also was a losing-oriented coach. He was fired midway through the 1973 season, and Svare was replaced by Tommy Prothro, a successful college coach at UCLA.

The team also had a new quarterback. In the 1973 college draft, the Chargers took Dan Fouts, who had starred at the University of Oregon. Fouts joined veteran John Unitas, who had come in a trade from the Baltimore Colts. John Hadl had been traded to the Los Angeles Rams. Fouts sat on the bench as first Unitas, and then James Harris were given a chance to lead San Diego. The Chargers, meanwhile, finished last in the AFC Western Division in 1973, 1974, and 1975.

In 1976 Prothro decided it was time to make Fouts the permanent starter. This eventually proved to be a very good decision. Fouts had shown NFL abilities for years, going back to his days as a young ball boy with the San Francisco 49ers. Vince Tringali, Fout's high school coach, noted Fouts's abilities even before the quarterback enrolled in high school. "A coach just naturally looks all over the field, and so I noticed this kid on the sidelines throwing the ball back to the referee," Tringali said. "I didn't know who he was, but I could see he had a heck of an arm."

Fouts, however, did not keep his starting position. Prothro often replaced him with James Harris. Both quarterbacks struggled despite the presence of several new offensive stars. Prothro used the Chargers' first-round draft pick in 1978 to take Arizona State wide receiver John Jefferson. Prothro also brought in another receiver, Charlie Joiner, thanks to a trade with the Cincinnati Bengals. The team had the ingredients for a great offense, but Prothro wouldn't be around to see the final result. After the Chargers opened the 1978 season with a victory over the Seattle Seahawks, the team lost three in a row. Prothro resigned, and owner Gene Klein brought in offensive wiz Don Coryell as the new coach. Coryell had made the St. Louis Cardinals into one of the most exciting teams in pro football. He loved the pass, and he wasn't afraid to use it at any time.

1 9 7 6

Rookie Charlie Joiner was the team's leading receiver, gaining over 1000 yards.

FOUTS BECOMES THE PILOT OF AIR CORYELL

After a loss to the New England Patriots, the Chargers rebounded to defeat Denver 23-0. It was the game that turned San Diego's season around. "There's a different kind of feeling on this team now," said Fouts, who was again the starter. "We feel like we're supposed to win every game. That's a big change when everyone expected us to lose." Suddenly, it was as if the Chargers had

The acrobatic Wes Chandler, (pages 18–19).

forgotten how to lose. Led by Fouts, the team won nineteen of its next twenty-six games during the 1978 and 1979 seasons.

July 12—the Chargers start training camp at the University of California at San Diego.

"We're only doing what we do because of Dan," Coryell said. "He has such a flexible mind. He doesn't have all the qualities you'd want in an ideal quarterback. He's not a runner. He's a fine athlete, but he doesn't have the speed. But he is very, very intelligent, and he is extremely competitive and tough mentally. A pro quarterback has to be one of the most courageous persons in sports. He has no chance to prepare himself for a hit the way a running back does. And he's not as big and sturdy. We have an awful time getting Dan to throw the ball away. He wants to take his chances in there."

Fout's style soon paid off. In 1979 he broke the NFL single-season passing yardage record when he threw for 4,082 yards. Fouts, who also tossed twenty-four touchdown passes, also was the AFC's most efficient passer, based on the NFL's quarterback rating system. Despite the glowing stats, former San Diego offensive coordinator Bill Walsh thought Fouts's best attributes were his leadership, courage, and ability to perform in the clutch. "It took his technical development for people to realize his other qualities—his assertiveness, his leadership, his intelligence," Walsh said. "And I'm not sure there is anyone as tough as he is in standing up to the rush. He is naturally courageous. If somebody asked me who the best clutch players were, I'd put Fouts in a category with [Terry] Bradshaw and [Roger] Staubach."

Fouts combined with John Jefferson, Charlie Joiner, and super rookie tight end Kellen Winslow to lead the Chargers to a 12-4 record in 1979, good for an AFC Western Division title. Running back Chuck Muncie gave San Diego an effective ground game to complement a passing attack that everyone was calling "Air Coryell." Said Fouts, "We're going to throw the ball, and we don't care who knows it." However, the Houston Oilers managed to shut down Air Coryell in San Diego's first playoff game. The Oilers won 17-14, and San Diego's best season in more than fifteen years was over.

The following season, Air Coryell started moving at supersonic speed. Fouts led the team to an 11-5 record, which was good for another division title. As good as the San Diego offense had been in 1979, when it scored the second most points in the NFL, the Charger attack was actually better in 1980. A lot of the credit went to Fouts, but he made sure his teammates felt appreciated. "Unlike some quarterbacks," said guard Ed White, many times an All-Pro, "Dan's ego is under control. When we score, no matter how, he's the first to congratulate the linemen. It makes up for some of the fan and media attention that goes elsewhere."

San Diego charged into the 1980 playoffs determined to reach the team's first Super Bowl. A victory over Buffalo allowed the Chargers to host the AFC title game against the rival Oakland Raiders. The teams had split two games during the regular season, each winning on its home field. A sellout crowd jammed San Diego's Jack Murphy Stadium to see the team's most important game since the mid-1960s. The Chargers took an early lead, but the Raiders roared back to claim a 34-27 victory.

Air Coryell was grounded, but only temporarily. The Chargers won the division title again in 1981, the team's third straight. Everybody knew about Fouts and the

1 9 7 9

Dan Fouts' 4,082 yards passing broke the record previously held by the one and only Joe Namath.

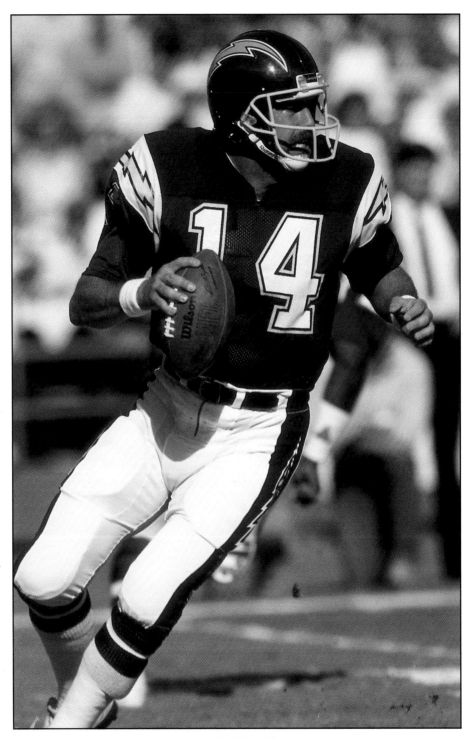

Quarterback Dan Fouts.

offense, but the San Diego defense was effective, too. Defensive linemen Louie Kelcher, Fred Dean, and Gary "Big Hands" Johnson applied the kind of pressure on quarterbacks that opposing teams could never seem to put on Dan Fouts.

In the first round of the playoffs, though, the defense had a rough time. The Chargers jumped to a 24-0 first-quarter lead against the Miami Dolphins. But Miami rallied for twenty-one points in the second quarter and actually took a 38-31 advantage in the fourth quarter. Then Fouts tossed a late touchdown pass to tie the game and send it into overtime. Winslow, who caught thirteen passes for 122 yards, made the biggest defensive plays of the game by blocking two Miami field goals. Finally, San Diego's Rolf Benirschke kicked the game-winner to give the Chargers a thrilling 41-38 victory. A week later in frigid Cincinnati, San Diego lost its second consecutive AFL title game, 27-7 to the Bengals. "I can't tell you how much it hurts to come this far and lose two years in a row," said a dejected Don Coryell.

The stadium was renamed for Jack Murphy, the late great sports editor of the San Diego Union.

JOINER CATCHES ON IN HIS THIRTIES

The Chargers wouldn't have a chance to play in a third straight AFC title game in 1982. The team made the playoffs, but lost to Miami in the second round. The next three seasons were hard on the Chargers. Defensive mainstays Fred Dean, Louie Kelcher, and Gary Johnson all left the club. Kellen Winslow suffered a horrible knee injury. Wide receiver Wes Chandler, who replaced the traded John Jefferson, was plagued by a series of injuries. So was

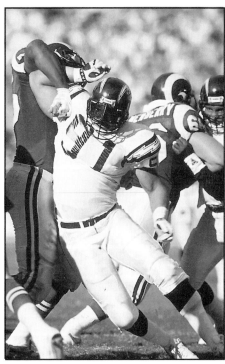

24   *Clockwise: Marion Butts, Billy Ray Smith, Leslie O'Neal, Kellen Winslow.*

Dan Fouts. Through all this adversity, there was one constant, one guy who was there no matter what—Charlie Joiner.

"I don't recall him ever missing a practice at all since I've been in San Diego," Coryell said. "One time, he cracked a rib and didn't take one day off. He said, 'I'll work through it.'" Said assistant coach Ernie Zampese of Joiner, "He honest to god believes that if you miss one practice, you'll lose something." Joiner not only practiced hard, he studied films and made sure he understood everything he could about defensive coverages.

Joiner, small at five feet eleven and 185 pounds, had some speed, but his mind was his biggest asset on the field. Bill Walsh called Joiner "the most intelligent receiver the game has ever known, the smartest, the most calculating. He could come off the field and tell me what had happened on the other side of the field," Walsh said. "He could get on the phone [to the coaches in the press box] and talk about coverages on the far side of the field. I don't know how he did it, a kind of extra sense, I guess."

Joiner became the Chargers' man to go to when the regular pass patterns broke down and when Fouts was being pressured in the pocket. In those cases, Fouts said, "all I'm trying to do is look for a port in the storm. He [Joiner] is the port. . . . Having Charlie is like having a fail-safe button. In our offense, it's up to me to decide who I'm going to go to, based on the coverages. When I'm back there in the pocket, I can tell when Charlie's going to be open, and at the last minute, I'll look to a spot and there he'll be. And he'll catch the ball."

Joiner credited Walsh for making him learn how to run proper pass patterns. "Coach Walsh taught me to work

1 9 8 3

Rolf Benirschke became the most accurate kicker in NFL history with an outstanding .720 field-goal percentage.

Veteran wide receiver Charlie Joiner averaged thirteen yards per reception.

within a disciplined system," Joiner commented. "I wasn't used to that kind of system. Everything was very precise under him."

Joiner's precise pass routes and his understanding of the coverages helped open up opportunities for San Diego's other receivers. After one game in 1984, a newspaper reporter asked Kellen Winslow why he was able to get open to catch ten passes that day. Winslow pointed toward Joiner's locker and said, "Ask him."

Ironically, Joiner didn't start to have seasons with a lot of catches until he was in his thirties. Most receivers see their productivity drop as they get older. Not Joiner. In 1984 he became the all-time leading pass receiver in NFL history, surpassing former Washington Redskin star Charley Taylor. When Joiner retired after the 1986 season, he had caught 750 passes for 12,146 yards, both NFL records. A year later, Seattle receiver Steve Largent broke those records, but Joiner remains second on the all-time receiving and yardage lists.

Joiner's last San Diego team was also the Chargers' worst season since 1975. The Chargers finished 4-12 in 1986. The days of Air Coryell were long gone. New coach Al Saunders tried to build the team around a strong defense. In spite of the Chargers' failures in 1986, two young defensive linemen had great years for San Diego. Lee Williams registered fifteen quarterback sacks, second most in the AFC. Leslie O'Neal had 12.5 sacks, which was fifth in the conference.

The improved defense and a healthy Dan Fouts keyed an 8-1 start in 1987. O'Neal was injured, but Williams, linebacker Billy Ray Smith, and cornerback Gill Byrd led the stingy San Diego defense. Everybody wondered what had happened to the once-lowly Chargers. Who were these guys? The Chargers rose to the dizzying heights of first place in the AFC Western Division, but they fell just as quickly. San Diego lost its last six games and wound up third in the division. It was the beginning of the end for Saunders, who was fired after a 6-10 season in 1988.

San Diego hired Dan Henning as coach in 1989, but the team had another losing record. However, after the 1989 season, the Chargers found a man who could prove to be the architect of San Diego's revival. His name is Bobby Beathard, and some experts call him the smartest man in football. As general manager with the Washington Redskins, Beathard rebuilt the team during the late 1970s and early 1980s, making Washington one of the best clubs in the NFL. Beathard, who quit the Redskins partly because he wanted to live in California all year, is San Diego's new general manager. He is responsible for finding the players to fill the team's weaknesses.

Despite some losing seasons, the Chargers do have some strengths. The defense is one of the youngest, but toughest, in the AFC. Lee Williams continues to be an excellent pass rusher. Leslie O'Neal has recovered from his injury and makes an ideal complement to Williams. Billy Ray Smith and Gill Byrd are other standouts. In addition, the Chargers are hoping defensive lineman Burt Grossman, the team's top draft choice in 1989, will mature into another quality player.

San Diego's recent problem, believe it or not, has been scoring. The team still hasn't found someone to replace Fouts, who retired after the 1987 season. But the team does have some weapons. Powerful fullback Marion Butts was one of the AFC's top rushers in 1989. Wide receiver

1 9 8 8

Tight end Kellen Winslow was named to the Pro Bowl for the fifth time.

Wide receiver Quinn Early.

Rising star Billy Joe Tolliver.

Anthony Miller has played well enough to be mentioned along with the team's great receivers of the past, guys such as Lance Alworth, John Jefferson, Wes Chandler, and Charlie Joiner. Tight end Rod Bernstein has drawn some comparisons to the now-retired Kellen Winslow. If young quarterback Billy Joe Tolliver continues to improve, the final piece in San Diego's puzzle for success may be in place.

The key to a long-sought championship, though, could be Beathard. His Washington teams were good enough to play in three Super Bowls during the 1980s, winning two of them. He turned down several other job offers to sign on with the Chargers. Beathard is a California fanatic who'd love more than anything else to mold San Diego into an AFC powerhouse. The man has a track record of success, and the Chargers are hoping Beathard stays on that course.